Make A Difference ... oice

Happiness ▪ Fear ▪ **Passion** ▪ Courage

WILLPOWER ▪ Gratitude ▪ GRIT

Opportunities ▪ Commitment

Storytelling ▪ **Goals** ▪ **Trust**

Pay the Price ▪ Obstacles ▪ Prepare

Circumstances ▪ **Achievement**

Inner Circle ▪ **Decide** ▪ Self Concept

RICHES ▪ Purpose ▪ Worry

Thoughts ▪ **INITIATIVE** ▪ DESIRE

Success ▪ ASK ▪ Reputation

Belief ▪ Change ▪ Time

Expectations ▪ COMFORT ZONE

Networking ▪ Risk ▪ **Determination**

324

To select the very best quotes,
more than 1,000 Quote Judges
from around the world
rated 1,005 quotes
for The Fired UP! Selling™ Project.

324
made the book.

"Everyone lives by selling something."

— ROBERT LOUIS STEVENSON

This book is
for everyone
who wants to live
a fired-up life.

A fired-up person
has a can-do attitude,
contagious enthusiasm,
boundless optimism,
a courageous heart,
and
phenomenal perseverance.

GREAT QUOTES

TO

INSPIRE • ENERGIZE • SUCCEED

Sunnyside Books
An Imprint of Bard Press
Austin, Texas

"There is a destiny that makes us brothers; none goes his way alone. What we put into the lives of others, comes back into our own."

— EDWIN MARKHAM

for
SPENCER HAYS

Who taught me
fired-up selling
and changed my life
forever!

— RAY BARD

Contents

1 Think **BIG**

2 Get **GOING**

3 Keep GOING

4 Make the SALE

5 **Succeed**

6 A **Stronger,** Better You

GROSS WEIGHT   750 lbs.
WING LOADING   1.47 lbs/sq.ft.

WRIGHT 4 CYLINDER WATER COOLED ENGINE
     BORE 4"
     STROKE 4"
     POWER, INITIAL 12 H.P.
     WEIGHT 160 lbs. dry

SEWED SEAM LINE CODE

----- LOWER WING SEAM
----- UPPER WING SEAM

FRONT SPAR IS JOINED
AT THIS LINE AND CAN
BE SEPERATED WHILE
REAR SPAR IS HINGED
ALONG SAME LINE

SEWED SEAM LINE
AT 45° TO SPAN

FABRIC LACING

Z Y

2" 13" 13" 11.75" RIB SPACING

13" 11.75" INBOARD RIB SPA

RIB SPACING SAME ON
LEFT WING EXCEPT AT
TIP (AS NOTED) - UPPER &
LOWER PANELS IDENTICAL
EXCEPT AT CENTER SECTION AS
SHOWN BELOW

WIRE RUNS FROM WING
WIRES TO END OF RIB,
AS A KEEPER. - SAVES
A PULLEY.

FOOTREST

RUDDER CONTROL
WIRES

LOWER
PROPELLER
BRACE WIRE
UPPER BRACE WIRE

CHAPTER ONE

Think
BIG

"We either make ourselves miserable
or we make ourselves strong.
The amount of work is the same."

— CARLOS CASTANEDA

• • •

"Attitude is your ultimate energy
source for a better life."

— BARBARA BABBIT KAUFMAN

Life isn't about waiting
for the storms to pass. It's about
learning how to

dance in the rain.

— VIVIAN GREENE

"You'll see it when you believe it."

— WAYNE DYER

• • •

"Sometimes your only available transportation is a leap of faith."

— MARGARET SHEPARD

• • •

"Don't get discouraged;
it is often the last key in the bunch
that opens the lock."

— ZIG ZIGLAR

"Whatever
your mind
can conceive
and believe
it can achieve."

— NAPOLEON HILL

"Believe **you can** and you're halfway there."

— THEODORE ROOSEVELT

"Make your choices reflect your hopes,
not your fears."

— NELSON MANDELA

• • •

"The future isn't a place that we're going to go,
it's a place that you get to create."

— NANCY DUARTE

• • •

"It is our choices that show us what we truly are,
far more than our abilities."

— J.K. ROWLING

"Life is choice.
All day, every day.
Who we talk to, where we sit,
what we say, how we say it.
And our lives become defined by our choices.
It's as simple and as complex as that.
And as powerful."

— LOUISE PENNY

"It's choice — not chance —
that determines your
destiny."

— JEAN NIDETCH

"The world needs dreamers
and the world needs doers. But above all,
the world needs dreamers who do."

— SARAH BAN BREATHNACH

• • •

"Too many of us are not living our dreams
because we are living our fears."

— LES BROWN

"If it doesn't scare you, you're probably not dreaming big enough."

— TORY BURCH

• • •

"Look closely at the present you are constructing. It should look like the future you are dreaming."

— ALICE WALKER

"Nothing is so contagious as enthusiasm."

—Samuel Taylor Coleridge

"For every sale you miss

because you're too enthusiastic,

you will miss a hundred because

you're not enthusiastic enough."

— ZIG ZIGLAR

"The biggest human temptation is
to settle for too little."

— THOMAS MERTON

. . .

"Expect the unexpected.
And, whenever possible,
be the unexpected."

— LYNDA BARRY

. . .

"If people are doubting how far you'll go,
go so far that you can't hear them anymore."

— MICHELE RUIZ

THINK BIG

"It isn't where you came from, it's where you're going that counts."

— ELLA FITZGERALD

"It is good to have an end to journey toward,
but it is the journey that really matters
in the end."

— URSULA K. LE GUIN

• • •

"A goal is a dream
with a deadline."

— NAPOLEON HILL

"Learn from yesterday,
live for today,
hope for tomorrow."

— ALBERT EINSTEIN

. . .

"Let's go invent tomorrow rather than
worrying about what happened yesterday."

— STEVE JOBS

"Live out of your imagination,
not your history."

— STEPHEN R. COVEY

• • •

"Your imagination is your preview of

life's coming attractions."

— ALBERT EINSTEIN

"If you
must doubt
something,
doubt your
limits."

—— PRICE PRITCHETT

"Don't let what you cannot
do interfere with what
you can do."

— JOHN WOODEN

• • •

"Many things are improbable,
only a few are impossible."

— ELON MUSK

"Life is like a ten-speed bicycle.
Most of us have gears we never use."

— CHARLES M. SCHULZ

• • •

"As long as you believe it is
impossible, you will actually
never find out if it is
possible or not."

— JOHN SEYMOUR

"If you want to keep your memories,
you first have to live them."

— BOB DYLAN

• • •

"Life itself is a privilege,
but to live life to the fullest—
well, that is a choice."

— ANDY ANDREWS

• • •

"You've gotta dance like there's nobody
watching, love like you'll never be hurt,
sing like there's nobody listening,
and live like it's heaven on earth."

— WILLIAM W. PURKEY

"Dream as if you'll
live forever.
Live as if
you'll die today."

— JAMES DEAN

"Life is like a coin.

You can spend it any way you wish,

but you only spend it once."

— LILLIAN DICKSON

"There are two ways of spreading **light**; to be the candle or the **mirror** that reflects it."

— EDITH WHARTON

"What you leave behind is not what is
engraved in stone monuments,
but what is woven into the lives of others."

— PERICLES

• • •

"If you think you're too small to have an impact,
try going to bed with a mosquito
in the room."

— ANITA RODDICK

• • •

"Don't count the days;
make the days count."

— MUHAMMAD ALI

"It was only a sunny smile,
and little it cost in the giving,
but like morning light
it scattered the night and
made the day
worth living."

— F. SCOTT FITZGERALD

"You miss 100%
of the shots
you don't take."

— WAYNE GRETZKY

"Opportunity is never lost . . . it simply
moves on to someone else
if you don't seize it!"

— KIM GARST

• • •

"Opportunity is missed by most people
because it is dressed in overalls
and looks like work."

— THOMAS EDISON

• • •

"You create opportunities by performing,
not complaining."

— MURIEL SIEBERT

"Optimism is the faith that leads to achievement."

— HELEN KELLER

. . .

"You cannot have a positive life and a negative mind."

— JOYCE MEYER

"There is no passion to be found
playing small — in settling for a life
that is less than the one
you are capable of living."

— NELSON MANDELA

• • •

"Working hard for something
we don't care about is called
stress; working hard for
something we love
is called passion."

— SIMON SINEK

"The two most important days in your life are the day you were born and the day you find out why."

—— MARK TWAIN

"When you walk with purpose,
you collide with destiny."

— BERTICE BERRY

• • •

"Life isn't about finding yourself.
Life is about creating yourself."

— GEORGE BERNARD SHAW

"You become what you
think about."

— EARL NIGHTINGALE

• • •

"If you don't like something, change it;
if you can't change it,
change the way you think about it."

— MARY ENGELBREIT

• • •

"Change your thoughts
and you change your world."

— NORMAN VINCENT PEALE

"Look at things not as they are,
but as they can be."

— DAVID J. SCHWARTZ

• • •

"Skate to where the puck is going to be,
not where it has been."

— WAYNE GRETZKY

*"Vision is the art of seeing
things invisible."*

—JONATHAN SWIFT

CHAPTER TWO

Get
GOING

"The way to get started is to stop talking
and start doing."

— WALT DISNEY

• • •

"You can't start at the
finish line."

— STELLA MONTANA

• • •

"All the fancy footwork is great.
But if you want to score, you have to shoot."

— ERIC COLE

"Action conquers fear."

— Peter Nivio Zarlenga

"A comfort zone is a
dangerous place."

— MARY LOU RETTON

• • •

"The risk of a wrong decision
is preferable to the terror
of indecision."

— MOSES MAIMONIDES

"Growth and comfort
don't coexist."

— VIRGINIA ROMETTY

"Too little confidence,
and you're unable to act;
too much confidence,
and you're unable to hear."

— JOHN MAEDA

. . .

"Half of getting there is having
the confidence to show up
and keep showing up."

— SOPHIA AMORUSO

. . .

"Confidence sells — people believe in
those who believe in themselves."

— SIMON BLACK

**"Confidence is quiet.
Insecurity is loud."**

— KARIN LUISE

"Confidence

is what happens

when you've done the hard work

that entitles you to

succeed."

— PAT SUMMITT

"The brave do not live forever,
but the cautious
do not live at all."

— MEG CABOT

• • •

"Courage is like a muscle.
We strengthen it by use."

— RUTH GORDON

"Often, in the real world, it's not the smart
who get ahead but the bold."

— ROBERT T. KIYOSAKI

· · ·

"Only those who will risk
going too far can possibly
find out how far one can go."

— T.S. ELIOT

"A ship in port is safe, but that's not what ships are built for."

—GRACE HOPPER

"The most difficult
thing is the decision
to act; the rest is
merely tenacity."

— AMELIA EARHART

"The most unprofitable item
ever manufactured is an excuse."

— JOHN MASON

• • •

"Excuses are the nails used
to build a house of failure."

— DON WILDER

• • •

"Some people have thousands of reasons why
they cannot do what they want to, when all
they need is one reason why they can."

— WILLIS R. WHITNEY

"When you summon the courage to travel
to the center of your fear, you often find
that there is nothing there."

— DEBORAH ROSADO SHAW

· · ·

"Fear lives in the head.
Courage lives in the heart."

— LOUISE PENNY

· · ·

"Use your fear, it can take you to
the place where you store your courage."

— AMELIA EARHART

"There are two ways to get to the top of an oak tree. One way is to sit on an acorn and wait; the other way is to climb it."

— KEMMONS WILSON

• • •

"The great thing about initiative is that it's free and available to everyone."

— MARIA BARTIROMO

• • •

"The journey of a thousand miles begins with one step."

— LAO TZU

"Take the first step in faith.
You don't have to see the
whole staircase, just take
the first step."

— MARTIN LUTHER KING, JR.

"Nobody cares if you can't dance well. Just get up and dance."

— DAVE BARRY

"People often say that motivation doesn't last. Well, neither does bathing — that's why we recommend it daily."

— ZIG ZIGLAR

• • •

"Everyone has to get good at one of two things: planting in the spring or begging in the fall."

— JIM ROHN

"If we wait until we're ready,
we'll be waiting for the rest of our lives."

— LEMONY SNICKET

. . .

"There are seven days in the week and
someday isn't one of them."

— SHAQUILLE O'NEAL

. . .

"You can't steal second base
and keep your foot on first."

— FREDERICK WILCOX

"If you risk
nothing
then you risk
everything."

— GEENA DAVIS

CHAPTER THREE

Keep GOING

"A bend in the road isn't the end of the road
unless you fail to make the turn."

— HELEN KELLER

. . .

"The pessimist complains about the wind;

the optimist expects it to change;

the realist adjusts the sails."

— WILLIAM ARTHUR WARD

"The real glory is being knocked to your knees and then coming back."

— VINCE LOMBARDI

"Rock bottom became the
solid foundation on which
I rebuilt my life."

— J.K. ROWLING

. . .

"You can't go back and make a new start,
but you can start right now
and make a brand new ending."

— JAMES R. SHERMAN

"There are only two options
regarding commitment:
you're either in or you're out.
There is no such thing as
life in-between."

— PAT RILEY

"Success doesn't come
from what you do occasionally;
it comes from what you do consistently."

— MARIE FORLEO

• • •

"The most important thing in life is
to stop saying 'I wish'
and start saying 'I will.'"

— CHARLES DICKENS

• • •

"If you're interested, you will do
what is convenient; if you're committed,
you'll do whatever it takes."

— JOHN ASSARAF

"Unrelenting action is what turns
starry-eyed daydreams
into steely-eyed objectives."

— ROY H. WILLIAMS

• • •

"What counts is not necessarily the size
of the dog in the fight — it's the size of the
fight in the dog."

— DWIGHT D. EISENHOWER

KEEP GOING

"You can blow out
a candle. But you
can't blow out a fire."

— PETER GABRIEL

"Failure is a bruise,
not a tattoo."

— JON SINCLAIR

. . .

"Failure is not the falling down,
but the staying down."

— MARY PICKFORD

"If you can't fly then run,
if you can't run then walk,
if you can't walk then crawl,
but whatever you do
you have to keep moving forward."

— MARTIN LUTHER KING JR.

• • •

"Being a professional is doing all
the things you love to do
on the days you don't feel like
doing them."

— JULIUS ERVING

*"No matter how you feel,
get up, dress up
and show up."*

— REGINA BRETT

"Luck is a word people who are lazy use to describe people who are hustling."

— JON ACUFF

"Coasting only takes you
downhill."

— ROGER CRAWFORD

• • •

"Even if you're on the right track,
you'll get run over if you just sit there."

— WILL ROGERS

"Always make new mistakes."

— ESTHER DYSON

• • •

"A man must be big enough to admit his mistakes, smart enough to profit from them, and strong enough to correct them."

— JOHN C. MAXWELL

• • •

"Own your mistakes. It shows confidence, accountability, and integrity."

— TRAVIS BRADBERRY

"The worst walls are never the ones
you find in your way.
The worst walls are the ones
you put there."

— URSULA K. LE GUIN

• • •

"If you break your neck,
if you have nothing to eat,
if your house is on fire,
then you got a problem.
Everything else is inconvenience."

— ROBERT FULGHUM

"Enthusiasm is common.
Endurance is rare."

— ANGELA LEE DUCKWORTH

. . .

"Don't assume a door is closed;
push on it.
Don't assume if it was closed yesterday
that it is closed today."

— MARIAN WRIGHT EDELMAN

"A river
cuts through
rock, not
because of
its power, but
because of its
persistence."

— JIM WATKINS

"Success is a little like wrestling a gorilla.
You don't quit when you are tired —
you quit when the gorilla is tired."

— ROBERT STRAUSS

"Quitting is a
permanent
solution
to a temporary
problem."

— RICHARD DE VOS

"If you only walk on sunny
days you'll never reach
your destination."

— PAULO COELHO

• • •

"Between peaks there are always valleys.
How you manage your valley determines
how soon you will reach your next peak."

— SPENCER JOHNSON

"The elevator to success is out
of order. You'll have to use the
stairs, one step at a time."

— JOE GIRARD

• • •

**"The man who removes
a mountain begins
by carrying away
small stones."**

— CONFUCIUS

"The
smallest
of actions is
always better
than the noblest
of intentions."

— ROBIN SHARMA

"You may not control all the events that happen to you, but you can decide not to be reduced by them."

— MAYA ANGELOU

• • •

"The tests of life aren't meant to break you but to make you."

— NORMAN VINCENT PEALE

• • •

"Storms make trees take deeper roots."

— DOLLY PARTON

"Make it a bad moment, not a bad day!"

— KATHERINE MYLIUS

"The **will to succeed** is important,
but what's more important is the
will to prepare."

— BOBBY KNIGHT

. . .

"Self-discipline is the ability
to make yourself do something
you don't necessarily want to do,
to get a result
you would really like to have."

— ANDY ANDREWS

CHAPTER FOUR

Make the
SALE

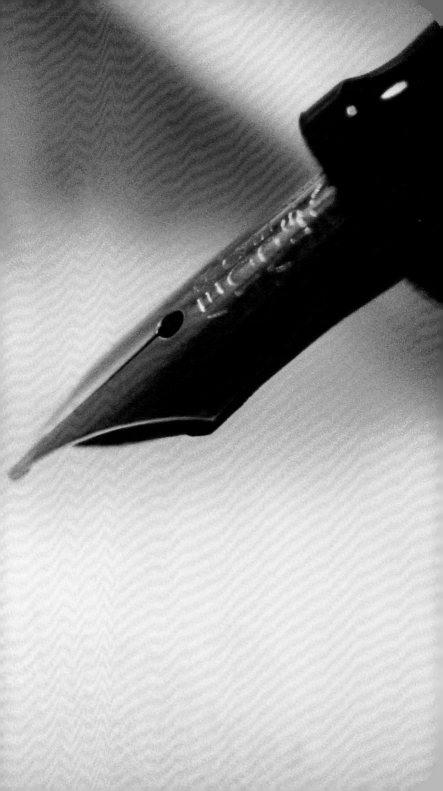

"If you don't ask, you don't give them the **opportunity** to say yes."

— JENNIFER GUE

• • •

"After you ask a closing question, SHUT UP! The next person who speaks loses."

— JEFFREY GITOMER

"The biggest challenge in business is not the competition, it's what goes on **inside your own head**."

— BARBARA CORCORAN

. . .

"Face-to-face contact will give you the edge over your competitors every time."

— JOANNE BLACK

"Compete with
yourself,
not with others."

— SOPHIA AMORUSO

"You can raise the bar or you
can wait for others to raise it,
but it's getting raised regardless."

— SETH GODIN

"There's only one boss:
the customer.

He can fire everybody
from the chairman on down
simply by spending his money elsewhere."

— SAM WALTON

"People don't just buy your products that they can see; they buy your attitude that they can sense."

— ROXANNE EMMERICH

• • •

"Our customers don't care about our problems, they care about their problems."

— MARK HUNTER

"Start working with
your prospects as if
they've already
hired you."

— JILL KONRATH

"Working a little harder to keep a customer now is a lot smarter than working a lot harder later to get a new customer."

— JILL GRIFFIN

. . .

"Every client you keep is one less that you need to find."

— NIGEL SANDERS

"The first step in exceeding your customer's expectations is to know those expectations."

— ROY H. WILLIAMS

• • •

"The most important secret of salesmanship is to find out what the other fellow wants, then help them find the best way to get it."

— CLAYTON M. HUNSIKER

"Wonder what your
customer really wants?
Ask. Don't tell."

— LISA STONE

• • •

"Nobody cares about your product, service
or solution. All they care about is the
difference you can make
for their organization."

— JILL KONRATH

MAKE THE SALE

"The customer's perception is your reality."

— KATE ZABRISKIE

"Good enough never is."

— DEBBI FIELDS

. . .

"The seven smartest words in
the English language are:
I don't know, but I'll find out."

— LARRY LUCCHINO

. . .

"Your most unhappy customers are your greatest source of learning."

— BILL GATES

"The man who does more than he is paid for
will soon be paid for more than he does."

— NAPOLEON HILL

• • •

"There are no traffic jams along
the extra mile."

— ROGER STAUBACH

• • •

"Here is a simple but powerful rule.
Always give people more than they expect."

— NELSON BOSWELL

"Act as though each
conversation is the most
important one you will
ever have. Because,
in that moment it is."

—GEMMA STONE

"No man ever listened himself out of a job."

— CALVIN COOLIDGE

. . .

"Most people think 'selling' is the same
as 'talking.' But the most effective salespeople
know that listening is the most
important part of their job."

— ROY BARTELL

. . .

"The quieter you become,
the more you can hear."

— RAM DASS

"One genuine new relationship is worth
a fistful of business cards."

— SUSAN CAIN

· · ·

"If you're the smartest guy in the
room, find another room."

— JAMES D. WATSON

"You can make more friends
in two months by
being interested in them
than in two years by
**making them interested
in you.**"

—DALE CARNEGIE

"To be persuasive, we must be believable.

To be believable, we must be credible.

To be credible,
we must be truthful."

— EDWARD R. MURROW

. . .

"The difference between the right word
and the almost right word is the difference
between lightning and a lightning bug."

— MARK TWAIN

. . .

"Your first ten words are more
important than your next ten thousand."

— ELMER WHEELER

"Maybe the reason it seems that price is all your customers care about is that you haven't given them anything else to care about."

— SETH GODIN

• • •

"When you sell on price, you are a commodity. When you sell on value, you are a resource."

— BOB BURG

"The questions you ask are more important than the things you could ever say."

—TOM FREESE

"You can tell whether a man is clever by his answers. You can tell whether a man is wise by his questions."

— NAGUIB MAHFOUZ

• • •

"Successful people ask
better questions,
and as a result, they get
better answers."

— ANTHONY ROBBINS

"Seek first to understand,
then to be understood."

— STEPHEN R. COVEY

"Remember, the universal language is not texted, emailed, or spoken. It is felt."

— ANGELA AHRENDTS

• • •

"Buyers do business with you, not with your company and not with technology."

— JOANNE BLACK

• • •

"Laughter is the shortest distance between two people."

— VICTOR BORGE

"People trust more,
listen more, buy more
when they learn about you
from someone they
respect and trust."

— JENNIFER GLUCKOW

"Every strike brings me closer to
the next home run."

— BABE RUTH

• • •

"Success is 99% failure."

— SOICHIRO HONDA

• • •

"If Plan A fails, remember that
you have 25 more letters."

— CHRIS GUILLEBEAU

"The best salesmen are those who are rejected most. They are the ones who can take any 'no' and use it as a prod to go on to the next 'yes.'"

— ANTHONY ROBBINS

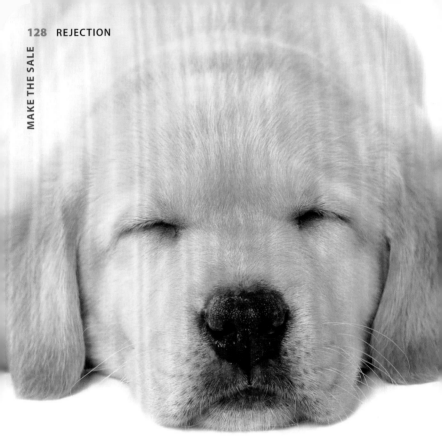

"Courage doesn't always roar.
Sometimes courage is
the quiet voice at
the end of the day saying,
'I will try again tomorrow.'"

— MARY ANNE RADMACHER

"Develop a reputation as a person who,
rather than talking a good game,
actually plays a good game."

— BOB BURG

• • •

"Begin somewhere; you cannot build
a reputation on what you intend to do."

— LIZ SMITH

"Treat your customers as though you were their most dedicated employee and consultant, ready to serve them in every way, so they feel your company is practically a division of their company."

— HARVEY MACKAY

· · ·

"Always give without remembering and always receive without forgetting."

— BRIAN TRACY

"If you walk in with information about you, they consider you a salesman.

If you walk in with ideas and answers, they consider you a resource.

Which one are you?"

— JEFFREY GITOMER

"At the end of the day, we are not selling,
we are serving."

— DAVE RAMSEY

. . .

"Make sure that the
best thing to happen
to your customer
today is you."

— CHRISTOPHER CHANSKI

"Facts tell. Stories sell."

— TOM SCHREITER

• • •

"People will remember stories long after
they have forgotten your bullet points."

— LAURIE BETH JONES

"A salesman cannot know too much,
but he can talk too much."

— FRANK BETTGER

. . .

"Silence is one of the great arts
of conversation."

— MARCUS TULLIUS CICERO

"One must
learn to be
silent just as
one must learn
to talk."

— VIRGINIA WOOLF

"If you're talking, you're just selling. If they're talking, they're buying."

— AMANDA JOHNS

"Nothing destroys trust faster than making
and breaking a promise. Conversely,
nothing builds trust more than
keeping a promise."

— STEPHEN R. COVEY

• • •

"You can't ask people to trust you.
It has to be earned by the things you do."

— JEFFREY GITOMER

"The best way to talk to your prospects is through the success of your customers."

— ALEX BARD

"Loyal customers,
they don't just come back,
they don't simply
recommend you,
they insist that their friends
do business with you."

— CHIP R. BELL

CHAPTER FIVE
SUCCEED

"Practice isn't the thing
you do once you're good.
It's the thing you
do that makes
you good."

— MALCOLM GLADWELL

"If you are content with the best you have done,
you will never do the best you can do."

— MARTIN VANBEE

• • •

"Doing your best is more
important than being the best."

— SHANNON MILLER

"Even the Lone Ranger
didn't do it alone."

— HARVEY MACKAY

• • •

"Seek out the wise ones,
the tough ones,
the ones you respect and can learn from.
Those who will encourage you,
challenge you,
and expect the best from you.
They will be your life changers."

— CHIP R. BELL

"Be strong enough to stand alone,
smart enough to know
when you need help,
and brave enough to ask for it."

— MARK AMEND

• • •

"Ask for help, not because you're weak,
but because you want to remain strong."

— LES BROWN

SUCCEED

"If you have an apple and I have an apple
and we exchange these apples,
then you and I will still each have one apple.
But if you have an idea and I have an idea
and we exchange these ideas,
then each of us will have two ideas."

— CHARLES F. BANNAN

• • •

"Making the simple complicated
is commonplace; making the
complicated simple, awesomely
simple, that's creativity."

— CHARLES MINGUS

"If you want something bad enough, you'll **find a way.** If not, you'll find an excuse."

— NICKI KEOHOHOU

"Winning isn't everything,
but wanting to win is."

— VINCE LOMBARDI

"Saying yes to everything
will kill you **slowly**
and **softly**."

— STEPHANIE MELISH

"It's not so much how busy you are,
but why you are busy. The bee is praised.
The mosquito is swatted."

— MARY O'CONNOR

• • •

"If everything is important,
then nothing is."

— PATRICK LENCIONI

• • •

"Saying no can be the ultimate self-care."

— CLAUDIA BLACK

"Doing the most
important thing is
always the most
important thing."

— GARY KELLER

"The more credit you give,
the better it reflects on you."

— GAIL EVANS

• • •

"The best investment with
the least risk and the greatest
dividend is giving."

— JOHN TEMPLETON

• • •

"When you focus on making a difference
in other people's lives,
your life is the one
that improves the most."

— ROXANNE EMMERICH

"The miracle is this:
the more we share
the more we have."

— LEONARD NIMOY

• • •

"Go out and do for others
what somebody did for you."

— RANDY PAUSCH

"Habits are hard
only in the beginning."

— GARY KELLER

• • •

"Habit is either the best of servants
or the worst of masters."

— NATHANIEL EMMONS

"You can't hire
someone else to do
your push-ups
for you."

— JIM ROHN

SUCCEED

"There are two kinds of people,
those who do the work
and those who take the credit.
Try to be in the first group;
there is less competition there."

— INDIRA GANDHI

"No one
ever drowned
in his own sweat."

— ANN LANDERS

• • •

"Hard work spotlights the
character of people:
some turn up their sleeves,
some turn up their noses, and
some don't turn up at all."

—SAM EWING

"It is not the mountain we conquer,
but ourselves."

— EDMUND HILLARY

"The price of anything is the amount of life
you exchange for it."

— HENRY DAVID THOREAU

. . .

"There are no shortcuts
to any place worth going."

— BEVERLY SILLS

SUCCEED

"Don't feel entitled to anything you didn't sweat and struggle for."

— MARIAN WRIGHT EDELMAN

"People will forget what you said, people will forget what you did, but people will never forget how you made them feel."*

— MAYA ANGELOU

*This quote was voted number one by the Quote Judges at the Fired UP! Selling™ Project.

"Business, like life, is all about how you make people feel. It's that simple, and it's that hard."

— DANNY MEYER

• • •

"It's very inexpensive to give a compliment."

— JOYCE MEYER

• • •

"Remember that a person's name is to that person the sweetest and most important sound in any language."

— DALE CARNEGIE

"Pretend that every
single person you meet
has a sign around his or her
neck that says
'Make me feel important.'"

— MARY KAY ASH

"There are two types
of people in the world.
Those who come in the
room and say,
'Well, here I am!'
and those who come
into the room and say,
'Ah, there you are!'"

— FREDERICK COLLINS

"It is better to look ahead and prepare
than to look back and regret."

— JACKIE JOYNER-KERSEE

• • •

"To be prepared is half
the victory."

— MIGUEL DE CERVANTES

• • •

"The best preparation for tomorrow
is doing your best today."

— H. JACKSON BROWN, JR.

"A dream written down
with a date becomes a goal.
A goal broken down into
steps becomes a plan.
A plan backed by action
makes your dreams come true."

— GREG S. REID

"Ideas are worth nothing
unless executed.
They are just a
multiplier.
Execution is worth
millions."

——STEVE JOBS

"We are not the sum of our intentions but of our actions."

— BRENDON BURCHARD

• • •

"If you only do the bare minimum, don't expect anything but bare minimum results."

— J. J. WATT

"There is a gigantic difference between
earning a great deal of money and
being rich."

— MARLENE DIETRICH

• • •

"Wealth is not about having
a lot of money.
It's about having
a lot of options."

— CHRIS ROCK

• • •

"Your income is determined by how
many people you serve and how well
you serve them."

— BOB BURG

"Success is about
doing the right thing,
not about
doing everything right."

— GARY KELLER

• • •

"To be responsible, keep your promises
to others. To be successful,
keep your promises to yourself."

— MARIE FORLEO

"Success is never owned;
it is only rented —
and the rent is due
everyday."

— RORY VADEN

"Yesterday is a cancelled check;
tomorrow is a promissory note;
today is the only cash you have —
so spend it wisely."

— KAY LYONS

. . .

"What we spend our time on
is the most important decision
we make."

— RAY KURZWEIL

"You are in business for yourself and your only inventory is TIME."

— ROY H. WILLIAMS

CHAPTER SIX

A Stronger
BETTER
You

"The biggest mistake we can ever make in our lives is to think we work for anybody but ourselves."

— BRIAN TRACY

· · ·

"We cannot change the cards we are dealt, just how we play the hand."

— RANDY PAUSCH

· · ·

"The only thing any entrepreneur, salesperson, or anyone in any position can control is their effort."

— MARK CUBAN

"You have brains in your head.
You have feet in your shoes.
You can steer yourself in any
direction you choose.
You're on your own, and
you know what you know.
**And you are the guy who'll
decide where to go."**

— DR. SEUSS

"No one can make you feel inferior without your consent."

—ELEANOR ROOSEVELT

"The most dangerous phrase in the
language is 'We've always done it this way.'"

— GRACE HOPPER

• • •

"God, grant me the serenity to accept
the things I cannot change, the courage
to change the things I can, and the wisdom
to know the difference."

— REINHOLD NIEBUHR

• • •

"Every day is a new opportunity
to change your life.
You have the power to say
'This is not how my story ends.'"

— KAREN SALMANSOHN

"When you're through changing, you're through."

— MARTHA STEWART

• • •

"Change before you have to."

— JACK WELCH

"**Stand** for something or you will fall for anything."

— ROSA PARKS

"The most exhausting thing
you can be is inauthentic."

— ANNE MORROW LINDBERGH

• • •

"Humility does not mean you think less of
yourself. It means you think of yourself less."

— KEN BLANCHARD

• • •

"Integrity is telling myself the truth. And
honesty is telling the truth to other people."

— SPENCER JOHNSON

"Don't impress others with what you have;
impress them with who you are."

— ROBERT TEW

• • •

"Hold yourself responsible for a higher
standard than anybody expects of you."

— HENRY WARD BEECHER

"I've never been poor, only broke. Being poor is a frame of mind. Being broke is only a temporary situation."

— MIKE TODD

"The situation you live in doesn't have to live in you."

— ROBERTA FLACK

· · ·

"Empty pockets never held anyone back. Only empty heads and empty hearts can do that."

— NORMAN VINCENT PEALE

· · ·

"Your present circumstances don't determine where you can go; they merely determine where you start."

— NIDO QUBEIN

"Be so good
they can't
ignore you."

— STEVE MARTIN

"Excellence is not a skill.
It's an attitude."

— RALPH MARSTON

• • •

"Good is the enemy of great.
That's why so few things become great."

— JAMES C. COLLINS

• • •

"We are what we repeatedly do. Excellence,
therefore, is not an act, but a habit."

— ARISTOTLE

"We don't need more to be thankful for,
we just need to be more thankful."

— CARLOS CASTANEDA

• • •

"The more difficult it is to reach your
destination, the more you'll remember and
appreciate the journey."

— SUSAN GALE

"As we express our gratitude, we must never forget that the highest appreciation is not to utter words, but to live by them."

——JOHN F. KENNEDY

"Act the way you'd like to be
and soon
you'll be the way you act."

— LEONARD COHEN

• • •

"A person's main asset is
themselves, so preserve and
enhance yourself."

— WARREN BUFFETT

"The expert in anything was once a beginner."

— HELEN HAYES

"Don't judge each day by the harvest you reap but by the seeds that you plant."

— ROBERT LOUIS STEVENSON

"Happiness is an inside job."

— WILLIAM ARTHUR WARD

• • •

"Find happiness by delivering it."

— CHRIS MURRAY

"Happiness is when what you think, what you say, and what you do are in harmony."

— MAHATMA GANDHI

"Success is empty if you arrive
at the finish line alone.
The best reward is to get there
surrounded by winners."

— HOWARD SCHULTZ

• • •

"If you run around with 9 losers
pretty soon you'll be
the 10th loser."

— LES BROWN

• • •

"It's better to walk alone than with a crowd
going in the wrong direction."

— DIANE GRANT

"Show me your _____,
and I'll show you your
_____."

— DANNY HOLLAND

"I never learned from a man
who agreed with me."

— ROBERT A. HEINLEIN

• • •

"If you think education is
expensive, try ignorance."

— HARVEY MACKAY

• • •

"It's what you learn after you know it all
that counts."

— JOHN WOODEN

"When you lose,
don't lose the lesson."

— DALAI LAMA

• • •

"Learn the rules like a pro,
so you can break them like an artist."

— PABLO PICASSO

"Done is better than perfect."

— SHERYL SANDBERG

. . .

"Instead of waiting for perfection,
run with what you do,
and fix it along the way."

— PAUL ARDEN

"I am careful not to confuse excellence with perfection. Excellence I can reach for; perfection is God's business."

— MICHAEL J. FOX

• • •

"The thing that is really hard, and really amazing, is giving up on being perfect and beginning the work of becoming yourself."

— ANNA QUINDLEN

"Don't let your want for perfection
become procrastination."

— DANIELLE LAPORTE

• • •

"Do what you can, with what you have,
where you are."

— WILLIAM MEEK WIDENER

"A year from now you may wish
you had started today."

— KAREN LAMB

• • •

"Don't let yesterday use up
too much of today."

— WILL ROGERS

• • •

"Ultimately, what we regret
is not failure, but
the failure to act."

— ADAM GRANT

"Don't get so busy making
a living that you forget
to make a life."

— DOLLY PARTON

. . .

"I'd rather regret the things I've done than
regret the things I haven't done."

— LUCILLE BALL

"The willingness to accept responsibility for one's own life is the source from which self-respect springs."

— JOAN DIDION

• • •

"Small-minded people blame others. Average people blame themselves. The wise see all blame as foolishness."

— EPICTETUS

"The first person you
lead is you."

— JOHN C. MAXWELL

"The most common way people give up their
power is by thinking they don't have any."

— ALICE WALKER

• • •

"Never undersell yourself unless
you want everyone else to."

— ELAINE DUNDY

• • •

"Reputation is what other people know
about you. Honor is what you know
about yourself."

— LOIS MCMASTER BUJOLD

"Don't let other people

tell you who you are."

— DIANE SAWYER

"The quality of your self-talk creates
the quality of your life."

— NICKI KEOHOHOU

. . .

"Talk to yourself like you would
to someone you love."

— BRENÉ BROWN

. . .

"Don't be too hard on yourself. There are
plenty of people willing to do that for you.
Love yourself and be proud of
everything that you do.
Even mistakes mean you're trying."

— SUSAN GALE

"Be careful how
you are talking
to yourself because
you are listening."

— LISA M. HAYES

"If you want to test your memory,
try to recall what you were worrying about
one year ago today."

— E. JOSEPH COSSMAN

• • •

"Too much attention on
problems kills our faith in
possibilities."

— PRICE PRITCHETT

• • •

"Worry is a misuse of the imagination."

— DAN ZADRA

"Worry does
not empty
tomorrow
of sorrow,
it empties today
of strength."

— CORRIE TEN BOOM

The Fired UP! Selling™ Project Story

The Beginning

Folding down book page corners, tabbing with sticky notes, highlighting magazines and newspapers, gleaning from the Internet, keying and cutting/pasting into a file on my hard drive. More than a decade ago I began collecting quotes. Words that spoke to me. Some were lyrical like poetry. Some had zing and punch. Others, plain, simple truth.

After a few years there was a huge file. With the idea of publishing these gems I did some online research. There were hundreds and hundreds of inspirational quote books. So, I gave up on another bright book idea.

But I continued to collect quotes. And, a few years later I thought — who really needs inspiration? Who, more than any other, would find these quotes valuable? Who sometimes needs a spark, a bit of wisdom, a little encouragement, or a shot in the arm? And often, nothing more than being reminded to act on what they already know.

My answer was salespeople and entrepreneurs. They're the ones swimming against the tide — aspiring to achieve invisible dreams and grand goals.

Back to online research, to see how many quote books there were for salespeople. A big surprise — zero! How crazy was that? The people who need quotes the most didn't have a resource tailored for them. I knew there was a need. People put quotes on their refrigerator doors and bathroom mirrors, carry them as a reminder, use them in speeches and team meetings, and encourage colleagues and friends in emails and social media. In short, they use quotes to fire up their teams, their friends — and themselves.

So, I decided to turn my hobby collection into a real book.

Then the serious work began. We created a framework with salespeople in mind, including quotes from great sales figures, past and present, giants of personal development, and seasoned sales experts — as well as people from all walks of life. A big Q — how many quotes in the book? I first thought thousands. Then, no — only the very best. Not a jumbo, ho-hum collection with a few good ones scattered here and there. It should be a book of diamonds — those sparkling quotes with lasting power and compelling value. Then the Q — how to select the best from the thousands on my hard drive? How to discover the diamonds? A huge dilemma!

The solution was to create a project. To ask salespeople — which are the diamonds? What a concept! Asking your customers what they want.

To create a special book I needed ongoing assistance from some sales insiders, working in the real sales world. Before the Project began I asked Melissa Lombard and Stephanie Melish to be my Brain Trust. They graciously agreed to offer their advice, ideas, and support. Each brought their own unique sales experience — and their fired-up attitude.

The Fired UP! Selling™ Project

With the experience of the Brain Trust, the Quote Judges, and my years in sales, the Project was launched for salespeople, offered by salespeople, with quotes voted on by salespeople.

People were invited to join the Project and vote on the quotes, as well as offer their comments, suggestions, and favorite quotes. We asked sales managers, salespeople, sales trainers, consultants, bloggers, and quote lovers to tell us which quotes were the best. More than 1,200 people, from around the world, signed up to be Quote Judges. They voted on 1,005 quotes and more than 100 images during the yearlong Project.

The Quote Judges rendered their Verdicts on a collection of quotes twice a week, answering the question — Is this quote OK, Good, or Great? The Verdicts for each quote were tallied and a Power Score generated. That's how we discovered the diamonds.

Our Goals

- Create an engaging book to inspire and energize — to help people succeed — to live a fired-up life.

- Include contemporary and classic sources with people from a wide variety of disciplines.

- Show women's contributions. Benefit from their experience and wisdom — break away from the usual fare of quotes from mostly old, dead, white guys.

- Make it easy for people to find what they need with a user-friendly subject index and author index.

- Mirror the positive, hopeful messages with an attractive visual experience of color photographs and images.

Our Criteria

As we screened quotes for the Quote Judges we were looking for four qualities:

Hope — optimism, encouragement, possibilities — they inspire!

Elegance — lyrical, poetic, memorable — they sing!

Truth — wisdom, principles, guidance — they teach!

Energy — punch, sizzle, snap — they pop!

Our Guidelines

- All quotes must have authorship. No anonymous ones.

- A 1% rule limiting the number of quotes from the same person. With 324 quotes, that meant no more than three from any one person.

- Formal names for the authors, without titles such as Dr., Ph.D., President, Reverend, or General. Only a few exceptions, like Dr. Seuss.

- Correct authorship was important. We spent many hours researching, but for some quotes it was a judgment call.

The Design

We had many discussions about the reader's experience, the book's look and feel — its personality.

Why not ask our expert advisors — the Quote Judges? We did — and learned that nature inspired them most, not their business environment. With that in mind we began our search for images. No hefty handshakes, leaping people giving high fives. No conference rooms, monitor screens, or cell phones. No pinstriped suits, high-heeled shoes, fast cars, or fancy watches.

Ongoing Inspiration

We also asked the Quote Judges how we could continue to inspire them. We didn't get any requests for coffee mugs or big posters! But they liked the idea of a quick daily shot in the arm. We added the 55 Second FireUP!™. It's a couple quotes and one-liners for early morning inspiration and fun. Here's the link if you want to sign up — it's free.

http://firedupsellingproject.com

Communication

If you want to get in touch with us at The Fired UP! Selling™ Project, please send your comments, suggestions, and favorite quotes to:

goodfolks@firedupselling.com

To learn more about the Project go here:

http://www.bardpress.com/main/book/6

I hope you enjoy the book — and get Fired UP!

—Ray Bard
  Fired UP! Selling™ Project Director
  Publisher, Sunnyside Books and Bard Press

The Quote Judges — The All-Stars

These people made this a unique and special project. Their voting provided us the critical information to select the very best quotes. Their ongoing comments and recommendations gave us ideas, guidance, and encouragement.

More than 1,200 people from around the world signed up to be Quote Judges. Over the yearlong effort they gave us their Verdicts on 60 collections — 1,005 quotes and more than 100 images. These are the steadfast ones, the regulars. They are truly All-Stars!

Shannon Adkins • Dave Akister • Luis Aleman • Cameron Alexander • Brandon Allen • Eric Anderson • Ski Anderson • Rob Arnold • Craig Arthur • Renee Asolas • A. D. Atkinson • J. Atkinson • Stefan Babeck • Jean Carpenter Backus • Fatai Badmus • Brad Baker • Brad Ballee • Vic Barbero • Shawn Bard • Vess Barnes • Chip R. Bell • Hugh A. Benham • Wray Betts • Ken Bittke • Mindy P. Bloom • Nancy L. Blum • Sara Pencil Blumenfeld • Steve Boehnlein • Christopher Bove • Charles J. Brand • William P. Brandt • Robert Otis Braudrick • H. W. Bud Brown • Paula Butler-Kay • Steve L. Byrd • Raymond Campbell • Chris Carey • James Carrasco • Sergio Carrasco • Clay Cary • Maryann Charbonneau • Jonny Chisholm • Jim Christensen • Kim Churack • Aaron Churchill • Kenrick Cleveland • Dave Cooley • Casey Craig • Jim Crawford • Al Creekmore • Mike Croccia • Felix Cruz • Gita Daryanani • Andrew De Boer • Diana Deaton • Anthony Dina • Alisen Dopf • Bill Duncan • Kyle B. Edmonds • Jamey Elliott • Krista Ellis-Smith • Lisa Elmore • Daniela Enache • Peri Erdmann • Jeremy Esser • Bonnie Etheridge • Rett Evans • Warwick John

Fahy • Lisa Faithorn • Rachelle Fender • Bob Ferrari • Sean Finell • Jim Fitzgerald • Stephen Flad • John S. Ford • Paul Ford • R. Jane Fraser • Scott Fraser • Chris French • Matt Friscia • Jeffrey Fry • Adrienne Gaboury • Joseph Garlington • Mickey Garrett • Howard Garthwaite • Elaine Gerber • Holly Gierard • Shelley Goldbeck • CJ Goldberg • Robb Grandt • Donn C. Gray • Michael Gray • John G. Graybeal • Michelle Greve • Jill Griffin • Georgia Rae Gromov • Dave Grosenheider • Ruth Groshon • Geno Gruber • Charles Guice • Liz Guthridge • Susan Guzman • Will Hackett-Jones • Daniel Hagerman • Ann R. Hair • Melvin D. Hall • Peter F. Hammond • David W. Handler • Timothy Harris • Travis Harris • Kent Hartzler • Dave Hathaway • Kurt Haug • Rick Havenridge • Dennis Hayes • Jack Heald • Julie Hein • Robin Ann Helenius • Chester Henry • Kelly K. Herren • John Hetherington • Art Hoerle • Djann Hoffman • Paul Hoke • Jacob Holub • Bill Hughes • Bob Hughes • Robert Humphreys • Karen Hurst • Bill Hyche • Robby Jackson • Mike Jenkins • Cinde Johnson • Stan Keenum • Michael Keesee • Heather Kelley • Chris A. Kelly • Lorne Kelton • Huntley Ketchen • Troy King • Timothy Kirk • Tim Kist • Jeffrey Klose • Richie Kluesener • Ellie Knight • Ronald Kobrya • Fred W. Koebel • Bobby Kountz • H. Kremers • Faith Kuczaj • Douglas Kuehn III • Bobby G. Kuykendall II • Beverly J. Lane • John Lasher • Jay Leigeber • Gordon Leighton • Tina Leverenz • Jennifer Lewis • Troy D. Lezotte • Allan G. Lie • Bob Lindberg • Melissa Lombard • Janice Lufkin Shea • Leslie MacDonald • Rob MacKay • John F. Maher • Janice Mars • Carla Marshall • Enio Mascherin • Dave Matthews • Mark Maurer • Jay Mayer • Steve McBride • Kimberly McDole • Jeff McElheran • Keith Mcelyea • Peter McFadden • Ed McGah • Thomas E. McGlothlen • Scott McKinney • Larry McLaughlin • Jack McManus • Regina McNamara • Dale Meermans • Stephanie Melish • Valerie Mercurio • Christine Mifsud • Andrea Wells Miller • Bob Miller • Eric James Miller • Samuel J. Mills • Jacqui Misener • Randy Miyake • Charlie Moger • Rick Molcan • Bill Montgomery • Joseph H. Moody • Ted

Morgan • Dan Morman • Nick Morris • Helen Murdoch • Rekha Murjani • John Murphy • Bryan Nangle • Marco Navarra • Carol Nelson • Richard Newman • Paul A. Nicholls Jr. • Rick Nicholson • Theresa Nolet • Paul Novack • Katie O'Connor • Alex Offer • Nancy Okragleski • Michael Ord • Matthew John Pahl • David Palmer • Stephen Palmer • Jay Papasan • Wendy Papasan • Patti Papez • Pranay Parikh • Carmen Parker • Joey Parker • Reinert Peterson • Les Petriw • Bob Phillips • Roger Pickett • Timothy P. Pickett • David Polis • Ray G. Powell • Debra Presnell • Robert Priest • Scott Provence • Joe Pruss • Dave Puntney • Janice Pyka • John Ralston • T. J. Ramirez • Wes Ramsay • Barb Reid • Murray W. Renner • Vitaliy Reutsky • Natascha Reynoso • Shane Richardson • Kay Roach • Cynthia Robbins • Gary L. Roberson • Kirk D. Ross • Carol Rudofski • Bryant Sandburg • Dan Sarazin • Todd Sattersten • Rochelle Schaffrath • Gary Schertzer • Tim Schimmel • Rod Schwartz • Kay Scott • Lisa Seaberg • Dan Seidman • Dennis Senac • Jeff Sexton • James Sharp • Dave Sheely • J. Van Simpson • Kevin Skaalure • Steve Sluka • Garth Smith • Susie Smith • Zac Smith • Donna Snapp • Lee Snook • Vera Snook • Don Snyder • Howard Sobel • Frank M. Sorokach • Jon Spoelstra • Mark Springer • Brandon Steiner • Marty Stevens • David W. M. Stiles • Gregg Stutts • Jim Swoboda • Jeffrey James Sylvestre • B. Symons • Michael Szapkiw • Dick Taylor • Marilyn Tedesco • David Thelen • Matthew Thies • Mark Anthony Thoma • Nancy Thomas • Ken Thomason • Carol Thompson • Sam Thompson • Robert Topping • Cameron Torstenson • Gabe Trahan • Dave Travis • Gerald Trees • Abbey Trone • Philea Urquhart • Shelley Wade • Machele Waid • Tom Wall • John Fielding Walsh • Dave Warawa • Stephanie Lane Ward • Dan Watts • Eric D. Webb • Will Webber • Tim Weko • Dennis Welch • Greg A. Wentzel • Jay Werth • Dan Westervelt • Jack Whitt • Brad Whittington • Vi Wickam • Clark H. Wigley • Pam Wiley • Steve Wilhelmy • Roy H. Williams • Cynthia Williamson • Steve Worden • Phil Wrzesinski • Steven J. Wunderink • Valerie Young • Josh Yudin • Melanie Zimney

Subject Index

Also see refers to other main headings that relate to the topic. Specific quotes that refer to a topic are listed by page number.

Author Index

Acknowledgments

Many people contributed to the making of this book. These few are the most notable.

Very Special People

Spencer Hays (July 14, 1936 – March 1, 2017) was a master salesperson, majority owner and Chairman of the Executive Committee of the Southwestern Company. For seven summers during my college years I worked under his leadership. Selling books, knocking on thousands of doors, earning college tuition, and learning life lessons. Spencer was my sales manager, teacher, mentor, and inspiration. He taught me enthusiasm, positive attitude, and perseverance—the foundation of fired-up selling. He believed in me when I doubted and encouraged me when I needed it the most. His business and financial achievements were extraordinary as were his contributions to the arts and education. But, they were small when compared to the difference he made in the lives of tens of thousands of young men and women. His teaching and encouragement deeply enriched our lives and made untold opportunities possible. His generous spirit is a lasting example for all who knew him. Without Spencer, you would not be holding this book. I am forever grateful.

Roy H. Williams is a wordsmith extraordinaire. The author of the bestselling *Wizard of Ads* trilogy, he is the co-founder, with his wife Pennie, of the renowned Wizard Academy. Through his company, Williams Marketing, and his marvelous weekly *Monday Morning Memo,* he is the force behind thousands of small business entrepreneurs achieving financial and personal success beyond their wildest imagination. Over the years it has been my great pleasure to benefit from and enjoy Roy's exceptional curiosity and enthusiasm for learning. From the very beginning he has been the book's and the Project's biggest fan and most enthusiastic supporter. A special thanks, Roy!

Jeffrey Gitomer is the king of sales. Through thousands of seminars and more than 800 issues of his awesome weekly *Sales Caffeine* e-zine he has taught innumerable people to sell with passion and success. He lives fired-up selling! His inspiring, entertaining, and real-world books have sold millions. It's has been my good fortune to publish four of Jeffrey's books, including the bestselling sales book of all time — *The Little Red Book of Selling*. When he learned about the Project he was immediately and enthusiastically supportive. Thank you, Jeffrey!

Todd Sattersten knows business books better than anyone. The co-author of *The 100 Best Business Books of All Time*, editor, marketer, book consultant, and co-founder of IT Revolution Press, he knows what it takes to create and market an extraordinary book. Long before the Project came into being, his questions, suggestions, and nudges gave me ideas, tools, and encouragement to bring my "hobby" book idea into being. Todd, thank you for being such a great listener, advisor, and friend!

BrainTrusters

Melissa Lombard is known far and wide for her intriguing project and blog *Coffee with a Stranger*. Her years of experience in sales and sales training were invaluable to the Project. Always curious and creative, while still in sales, she continues to pursue her own unique adventures.

Stephanie Melish is the Double-Tall, Non-Fat, No-Whip Sales Barista. A professional speaker, success coach, and Gitomer Certified Trainer, she knows the sales and business world. Her blog *Straight Talk* and her book *Bank Your Mistakes* inform, challenge, and inspire.

These two friends were amazingly helpful. Sales insiders, working in the real, everyday sales world, they graciously gave me ideas, and support. Throughout the Project they were wonderful advisors and cheerleaders, helping make it a better book. Always available for numerous quick-turn requests, they were fired-up from the beginning. Many, many thanks Melissa and Stephanie!

The Home Team

These are the unsung ones, the ones behind the scene who did the work. **Sherry Todd,** serving as project manager, got us off the ground and skillfully managed us through all the deadlines and Survey Monkey glitches. **Deborah Costenbader** was there from the beginning to the end, tracking, researching and verifying quotes. And then helping me pull it all together with her organizational expertise and patience. **Kimberly McDole** joined the Project when I needed help the most and provided excellent research and organizational assistance. **Gary Hespenheide** and **Randy Miyake** at Hespenheide Design in Los Angeles provided their usual great creative design and production services. For more than 15 years they've allowed me to tinker and act like I know more about design than they do. This time they went beyond their usual fine work. **Joe Pruss,** the author services and operations manager at Bard Press, as he has for many years, provided great support for the Project from beginning to end.

I'm most grateful for all their help and support.

— Ray Bard

Photo Credits

page 7, © ilolab/Shutterstock; **page 12,** blueprint drawing courtesy of Wright Brothers Aeroplane Company at wright-brothers.org, © Brad Whitsitt/Shutterstock; **page 15,** © Michal Bednarek/Dreamstime; **page 17,** © Algol/Dreamstime; **page 18,** Library of Congress; **page 22,** © Sam Sherman/Dreamstime; **page 29,** © Keystone Pictures USA/Alamy Stock Photo; **page 33,** © joecicak/iStock; **page 37,** © gongzstudio/123RF; **page 39,** © Olga Olejnikova/123RF; **page 41,** © Igor Chaykovsky/123RF; **page 42,** © Serg Zastavkin/Shutterstock; **page 47,** Public Domain; **page 51,** © Greg Rakozy/Unsplash; **page 52,** © DLILLC/Corbis/VCG; **page 57,** © Tatyana Tomsickova/Alamy; **page 63,** © guita22/123RF; **page 65,** © Hulton Archive/Getty Images; **page 69,** © ehrlif/Shutterstock; **page 70,** © Ondřej Prosický/123RF; **page 73,** © Ammit Jack/Shutterstock; **page 74,** © Pixabay; **page 77,** © Jim Brandenburg/Minden Pictures/Getty Images; **page 79,** © Peter Beavis/Getty Images; **page 82,** © Ray Bard; **page 85,** © SCPhotos/Alamy; **page 86,** © ViktorCap/iStock; **page 91,** © Zack Frank/Shutterstock; **page 93,** © Tom Grundy/123RF; **page 96,** © Ray Bard; **page 98,** Galushko Sergey/Shutterstock; **page 100,** © Comstock/Getty Images; **page 104,** © UpperCut Images/Alamy Stock Photo; **page 108,** © LunarVogel/Shutterstock; **page 115,** © Kevin Eaves/Dreamstime; **page 123,** Lorna Roberts/Shutterstock; **page 127,** © Balz Bietenholz/Alamy; **page 128,** © Viorel Sima/Shutterstock; **page 131,** © SantiPhotoSS/Shutterstock; **page 135,** © Winnu/GATA; **page 140,** © Galyna Andrushko/Shutterstock; **page 142,** © Fogen/Shutterstock; **page 147,** © Drew English/Alamy; **page 149,** © phive/iStock; **page 151,** © Aliaksandr Mazurkevich/Dreamstime; **page 155,** © all-free-download.com; **page 158,** © Easyturn/iStock, Roberto Caucino/Shutterstock; **page 161,** © Ray Bard; **page 164,** © Shawn Hempel/Dreamstime; **page 167,** © sergign/Shutterstock; **page 173,** © DutchScenery/iStock; **page 174,** © Joerg Hackemann/123RF; **page 178,** © Apostrophe/Shutterstock; **page 181,** © piskunov/Getty Images; **page 186,** © Toria/Shutterstock; **page 189,** 18870020330/Shutterstock; **page 191,** © Dmytro Panchenko/123RF; **page 192,** © Max Smirnov/Shutterstock; **page 194,** Public Domain; **page 197,** © Nathan White Images/Shutterstock; **page 206,** © jahmaica/123RF; **page 208,** © JodiJacobson/Getty Images; **page 210,** © Photosiber/Shutterstock; **page 212,** © A. Singkham/Dreamstime

Fired UP! Selling™
Great Quotes to Inspire, Energize, Succeed
Ray Bard

Published by Sunnyside Books, an imprint of Bard Press, Austin, Texas

Ordering Information
For additional copies contact your favorite bookstore or
goodfolks@firedupselling.com. Quantity discounts are available.

ISBN
13 digit: 978-1-885167-83-5 ——10 digit: 1-885167-83-0

Publisher's Cataloging-in-Publication Data
Bard, Ray, compiler.
Fired UP! Selling™: great quotes to inspire , energize , succeed / [compiled by
Ray Bard].
Includes indexes. | Austin, TX: Sunnyside Books, an Imprint of Bard Press, 2017.
ISBN 978-1- 885167-83- 5
LCSH Selling--Quotations, maxims, etc. | Success. | Motivation. | BISAC
LCC HF5438.25 .B342 2017 | DDC 658.85--dc23

A Sunnyside Book
Credits
Project Manager: Sherry Todd
Copyeditor/Production Editor: Deborah Costenbader
Researcher: Kimberly McDole
Proofreading: Luke Torn
Text Design: Hespenheide Design
Text Production: Hespenheide Design
Jacket Design: Hespenheide Design
Index: Kay Banning

First Edition
First printing: May 2017

Get Fired UP!

Sign up for 55 Second FireUP!™

2 Inspirational Quotes and 2 Fun One-liners
delivered to your mailbox early Monday through
Friday mornings.
Sign up here: www.firedupsellingproject.com

Get More Copies of Fired UP! Selling™

Visit your favorite bookstore

or

Visit our website
http://www.bardpress.com/main/book/6

Big Quantity Discounts Available
As low as $5.99 per book.

Communicate with us at the
Fired UP! Selling™ Project

goodfolks@firedupselling.com

A Sunnyside Book—An Imprint of Bard Press
Austin, Texas

Attitude ▪ Enthusiasm ▪ Persistence

Listening ▪ Act ▪ **Motivation**

Comeback ▪ **Serving** ▪ Small Steps

Tough Times ▪ **Confidence**

Imagination ▪ EXTRA MILE ▪ Questions

Rejection ▪ Givers Gain ▪ Hope

Results ▪ Excuses ▪ **Serving**

Self Talk ▪ **Perfection** ▪ Character

Captain of Your Ship ▪ Optimism

Procrastination ▪ **Failure** ▪ **Dreams**

Focus ▪ Living All Out ▪ Mistakes

Hustle ▪ LIMITS ▪ Quitting ▪ Habits

Talking Too Much ▪ Hard Work

Excellence ▪ **Responsibility** ▪ Vision